BULLY BUSTERS AND BEYOND!

9 treasures to
self-confidence, self-esteem
and strength of character

MASTER PHIL NGUYEN

MorganJames
The Entrepreneurial Publisher™

NEW YORK

Bully Busters and Beyond!
9 Treasures to Self-Confidence, Self-Esteem, and Strength of Character

Published in New York, New York, by Morgan James Publishing. Morgan James and The Entrepreneurial Publisher are trademarks of Morgan James, LLC. www.MorganJamesPublishing.com

The Morgan James Speakers Group can bring authors to your live event. For more information or to book an event visit The Morgan James Speakers Group at www.TheMorganJamesSpeakersGroup.com.

A **free** eBook edition is available
with the purchase of this print book.

CLEARLY PRINT YOUR NAME ABOVE IN UPPER CASE

Instructions to claim your free eBook edition:
1. Download the BitLit app for Android or iOS
2. Write your name in **UPPER CASE** on the line
3. Use the BitLit app to submit a photo
4. Download your eBook to any device

ISBN 978-1-63047-381-5 paperback
ISBN 978-1-63047-382-2 eBook
ISBN 978-1-63047-383-9 hardcover
Library of Congress Control Number:
2014946308

Cover Design by:
Kathi Dunn
www.dunn-design.com

Illustrations by:
Erick Euler

In an effort to support local communities, raise awareness and funds, Morgan James Publishing donates a percentage of all book sales for the life of each book to Habitat for Humanity Peninsula and Greater Williamsburg.

Get involved today, visit
www.MorganJamesBuilds.com.

Habitat for Humanity®
Peninsula and
Greater Williamsburg
Building Partner

For my children and ninja sons, Justice and Jackson,
I love you with all my (martial) heart

For the children of the world – know that you are loved

Introduction by Master Phil

My first experience with bullying started when I was in grade school, as I was a victim of racial and psychological bullying.

When I became a parent, my #1 fear was for my children to become victims of bullying.

One day, my wife Amelia and I co-created our Bully Busters program based on our background in martial arts education, conflict resolution, and positive motivation to help victims become victors.

Today, you are holding in your hands this children's picture book to help your family come from a place of love, strength, and empowerment when faced with bullying and adversity.

It is children's tender hearts that should inspire us to be more and to do more with our days and with our lives.

I hope you read this book with your children (or students) regularly as an opportunity to build a powerful loving bond, to discover their 9 treasures within, and to remind them that they are destined for greatness.

For information on my presentations, resources, video training course, and to obtain your FREE Bully Busters Action Guide, visit: www.bullybustersandbeyond.com

I bow to your awesomeness.

Master Phil Nguyen

Sooooo...

It all begins and ends with respect

Respect yourself

even if you're not perfect

2

Respect other people,
always try to connect
Respect the environment,
it's ours to protect

3

Treat others the way that
they would expect
Learn wisdom of the elders
to make you reflect

Listen to your parents
they're usually correct
Loving yourself is
the best project

Fitness in Your Body

Soooooo...
You have to take care of
your precious body
Eat healthy foods
instead of candy

Sleep well at night
so you wake up happy
Train in martial arts,
do it with your family

7

Breathe in and breathe out
just like a yogi
Run outside, do push-ups,
or play hockey

You'll feel awesome,
full of energy
Take care of yourself,
you won't be sorry

Toughness in Your Mind

Sooooo...
Believe in yourself,
make your mind strong
Leaders are readers
and learning is lifelong

Focus on the positive
and it won't be long
Until you realize
that you belong

Bully words and actions
can hurt like a loud gong
But you know the difference
between right and wrong

Remember someone loves you
so don't prolong
Raise your hands high and
sing this song

Assertiveness in Your Behavior

Sooooo...

Walk with confidence and keep your back straight

Shake hands firmly and smile at your mate

Your eyes looking up and
let me re-state
Keeping good posture
is really great

15

When bullies try to hurt,
you'll have a higher heart rate
Stand up for yourself
and try to relate

Speak out for yourself
and communicate
Feeling strong and
proud is your ideal state

Kindness in Your Actions

Sooooo...
Be kind to others and try
to have compassion
Make others feel welcome
and show your dedication

To get along, make friends,
and build co-operation
Opening doors is polite,
a sign of consideration

19

Even when others aren't nice,
control your emotions
Caring about other's feelings
brings everyone satisfaction

Saying please and thank you
is a sign of affection
Helping others feel good,
is a positive action

Braveness in Your Heart

Sooooo...
When you lose,
raise your head with dignity
When you win,
bow your head in humility

When you make a mistake
or you're feeling lonely
Stand up and be brave
and take responsibility

23

When life is hard,
remember your ability
To listen to your heart
and act with integrity

Be true to yourself
for all of eternity
And you will enjoy a
life of prosperity

Boldness in Your Dreams

Sooooo...
Have a great life
and dream the big dream
Even though to some,
it might sound extreme

With courage and heart
and the right team
Living with passion
will be your theme

27

Create something beautiful,
that is your scheme
It might be scary,
you may want to scream

Your imagination will reign supreme
You're the hope of humanity,
a miracle machine

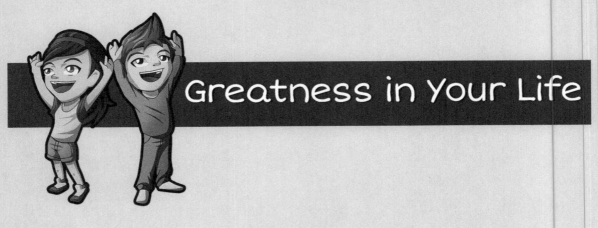

Greatness in Your Life

Sooooo...
Smile and breathe, go for happiness

Laugh, run, and have fun,
live with joyfulness

Say you're sorry and show forgiveness
Be honest with your words and
speak only truthfulness

On your quest to be your best,
remember thankfulness
Say a prayer every day,
to show your faithfulness

I love you my child,
and bow to your awesomeness
Use your might for right,
you are destined for greatness

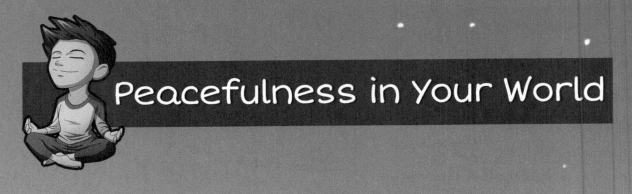

Peacefulness in Your World

Sooooo...

Have peace in your heart,
and always be loving

Every day and every way,
you're like a flower blooming

34

Keep our planet beautiful,
so the sun can keep rising
In your fellow man,
keep on believing

You can make a difference,
and help with the healing
Open your mind,
to a greater understanding

A more peaceful world,
you will be building

With your every breath,
you will lead a life of meaning

Thankfulness for Others

I bow to the awesomeness of the following people for their influence on, contribution to, and support of Bully Busters and my life's journey:

My family – for your love and support

My friends – for your encouragement and joy

My mentors – for your wisdom and guidance

My martial arts family – for your inspiration and dedication

My Kickstarter supporters – for your backing and belief in me

CPSIA information can be obtained at www.ICGtesting.com
Printed in the USA
LVOW01s2140021214

416801LV00003B/5/P